Fact Finders®

DISGUSTING JOBS IN MODERN AMERICA
THE DOWN AND DIRTY DETAILS

BY JACQUE SUMMERS

Content Consultants:
Chapulina Ramos, Wastewater Collection and Treatment Professional

Glenn Hardin, Professor of Practice of Forensic Science
Hamline University

Michelle Rippy, Assistant Professor
California State University East Bay

CAPSTONE PRESS
a capstone imprint

Fact Finders Books are published by Capstone Press,
1710 Roe Crest Drive, North Mankato, Minnesota 56003
www.mycapstone.com

Copyright © 2018 by Capstone Press, a Capstone imprint. All rights reserved. No part of this publication may be reproduced in whole or in part, or stored in a retrieval system, or transmitted in any form or by any means, electronic, mechanical, photocopying, recording, or otherwise, without written permission of the publisher.

Cataloging-in-publication information is on file with the Library of Congress.
978-1-5435-0366-1 (library binding)
978-1-5435-0370-8 (ebook PDF)

Editorial Credits
Editor: Alyssa Krekelberg
Designer: Maggie Villaume
Production specialist: Laura Manthe

Photo Credits
iStockphoto: anthonysp, 15, blisken, 28, digicomphoto, 20, fergregory, 5 (bottom middle left), genesisgraphics, 27, gsagi, 14, KatarzynaBialasiewicz, 17, 18–19, michaeljung, 24, Prathaan, 16, RichLegg, 21, xmee, 5 (bottom left); Shutterstock Images: Aliaksei Smalenski, 12–13, Avatar_023, 6–7, Brandon VandeCaveye, cover (top), Gena Melendrez, 10, kotoffei, 5 (road), Maceofoto, 25, Pakhnyushchy, 11, Pixel 4 Images, 22–23, Rich Stock, 29, Sanit Fuangnakhon, 8, serato, cover (bottom right), StockSmartStart, 5 (top right), 5 (top middle left), 5 (middle right), 5 (bottom right), travelview, cover (bottom left), Vladimir Mulder, 9, ymphotos, 5 (top left)

Design Elements: iStockphoto, Shutterstock Images, and Red Line Editorial

Printed and bound in Canada.
010800S18

TABLE OF CONTENTS

Introduction
WHO DOES THESE DISGUSTING JOBS? 4

Chapter One
FOUL FECAL MATTER 6

Chapter Two
DEATH AND DECAY 14

Chapter Three
BLOOD AND BONES 18

Chapter Four
PROCESSING MEAT 22

Chapter Five
HANDLING DEAD ANIMALS 26

Conclusion
THE WORKERS OF TODAY 29

Glossary 30
Read More 31
Internet Sites 31
Critical Thinking Questions 31
Index 32

INTRODUCTION

WHO DOES THESE DISGUSTING JOBS?

Where do urine and poop go once they are flushed? What happens to a body when a person dies? Who clears dead animals off the road? There are many workers who handle these tasks. **Sewer** workers climb through sewers filled with filthy, smelly water. Physicians cut open dead bodies. Roadkill collectors scrape flattened animals off the road. Despite advancements in technology people still must do disgusting jobs in modern America.

1920s
Only one in 10 homes has indoor plumbing. Most poop and urine go into the closest river or into holes near homes

1930s
Embalmers are required to have a license to work in any state

1940s
Crime scene **investigator** (CSI) becomes a job in big cities

1950s
New rules are introduced on how animals can be killed for food

1970s
New rules are made to protect people in the places where they work. These rules are important for people who work in dangerous locations, including sewers and factories

2000s
CSIs use devices to do things like find dead bodies. They also locate the labs where chemical weapons are made

2010s
Now, 99 out of 100 homes have plumbing

sewer — systems of underground pipes, tubes, and tunnels that connect together to move poop away from where people live
investigator — person who looks for clues to solve a mystery

CHAPTER ONE

FOUL FECAL MATTER

After it is flushed away, where does poop go? It flows down the toilet. Then it goes into underground tubes, pipes, and tunnels. These passages lead to a **wastewater treatment plant**.

wastewater treatment plant — facility where pollutants are taken out of dirty water

Some engineers at wastewater treatment plants manage projects.

7

DEAR DIARY

"In a sanitation sewer pipe . . . roaches are everywhere. Sometimes the manhole walls and pipes are covered with them: writhing, running, living walls of roaches."

—Chapulina Ramos, wastewater collection and treatment professional, 2017

The tunnels are watched by sewer workers. These men and women make sure the river of poop, urine, and toilet paper flows smoothly, but workers have to deal with more than just poop and urine. They clear away all items that shouldn't have been flushed down the drains. Moldy leaves, rotting dead animals, and cigarette butts are just some of the trash they find. Workers clear away clumps of paper, poopy diapers, and other garbage.

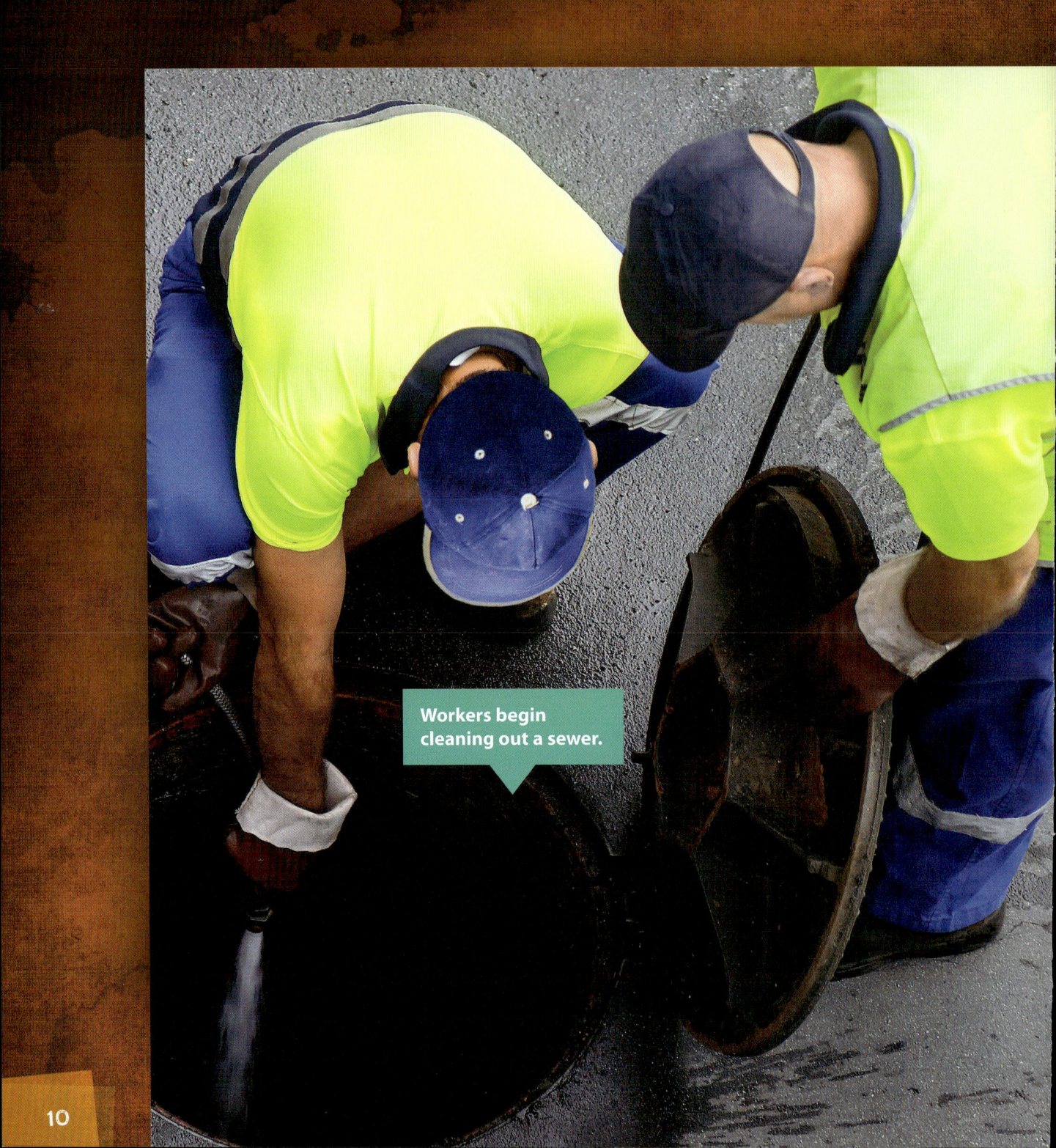

Workers begin cleaning out a sewer.

FOUL FACT

Sewer workers are at risk of getting many diseases. One disease is **leptospirosis**. It's caused by rat urine. People who get this disease vomit, turn yellow, and sometimes even die.

To get to the clogs, the workers climb down into the sewers. They spend the day kneeling, crouching, and crawling through tunnels. The smell of decay sticks to the workers' uniforms. They share the sewers with rats. They also see snakes and giant cockroaches. Sometimes the tunnels flood. All the poop and urine comes up out onto the street. Then they must clean it up.

leptospirosis — bacterial disease that humans can get from animals

FOUL FACT

An average human makes 77 pounds (35 kilograms) of poop and 132 gallons (500 liters) of urine each year. Human poop is sometimes used to fertilize crops eaten by cows and other animals. And animal poop is used to fertilize crops consumed by humans.

Tanks are used to treat wastewater.

The river of dirty water goes to the treatment plant. Poop is taken out of the water. It is dried and treated. Workers add chemicals to the water. This kills harmful bacteria. The cleaned liquid is pumped into a river, lake, or ocean. Some communities reuse the water to grow grass. They also use it to grow crops that are fed to animals.

CHAPTER TWO

DEATH AND DECAY

a shell casing from a bullet

When someone dies because of a crime, CSIs are called. CSIs arrive at the scene and go to work. They look for any **evidence** of the crime. This evidence can be blood, spit, and soil. It can be a shred of a fingernail. The evidence can be as small as a piece of hair. Whatever it is, the investigators need to find it. They hunt for bullets and other evidence. Sometimes they must dig through mud and garbage. Investigators rip up floors. They search ceilings and they dig in car trunks.

evidence — anything that can give a clue as to how an event happened

Every item of evidence that is found must be documented. Once the evidence is found, a marker is placed next to it.

The investigator makes a report, then he or she waits for another report from the medical examiner. Medical examiners use the dead body to find clues. They do this by cutting open the body. They record what they find.

FOUL FACT

In the medical examination room, blood that is drained from dead bodies flows down into a drain on the floor and into the sewer system.

At the crime scene, a team is hired to clean up. Blood may cover the walls and furniture. It may be in puddles on the floor, but the crime scene cleanup team must remove it. They get down on their hands and knees. They scrub every corner of the room.

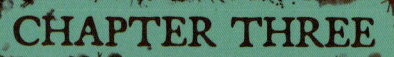

CHAPTER THREE

BLOOD AND BONES

Part of the work of a coroner is moving bodies to a **morgue**. Coroners also decide if an **autopsy** is needed. They are called by the police or by a hospital when they need to deal with a dead body. The longer a body sits, the smellier and more decayed it becomes.

morgue — place where dead bodies are taken and stored; here they are either examined or sent to the embalmer to prepare for burial

autopsy — when a body is cut open and studied to find out what caused the person's death

DEAR DIARY

"We went to work when the coroner called. It might be two o'clock in the morning and we had to go out. The smell is something I will never forget. A dead human body smells different from anything else I have ever smelled, and it created a feeling of fear in me almost instantaneously. But, we had to get the job done."

—*Steven Ignacio, coroner's assistant,* 2010

Sometimes the body is oozing green, yellow, or black liquids. This liquid is made up of old blood and green bile from the guts.

When the body needs an autopsy, investigators call a medical examiner who is a physician who specializes in autopsies. First the physician must undress the body. Then he or she washes it with soap. The physician cuts the body open. The smell of rotting flesh fills his or her nostrils. He or she pulls out the guts. The physician feels around inside the chest cavity for evidence as to how the person died. Then, he or she sews the body back up.

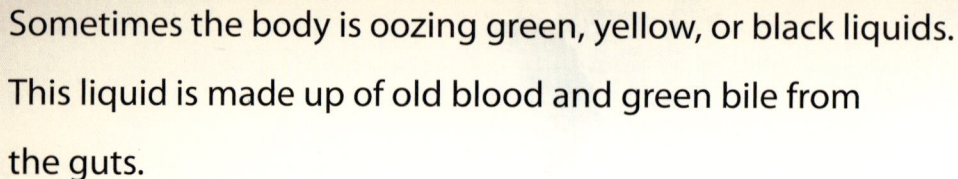

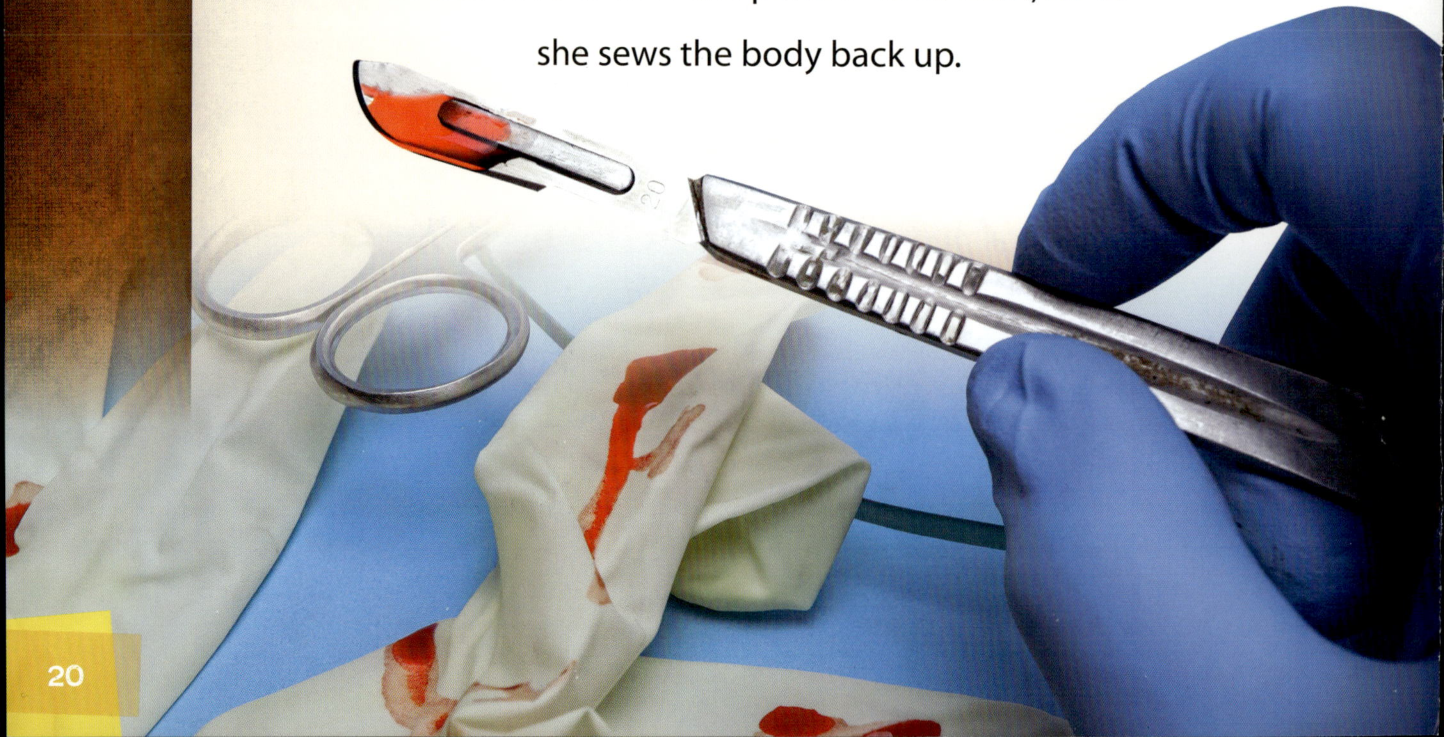

Embalmers arrange bodies for funerals.

Embalmers work at funeral homes. They prepare the body for burial. They insert a needle under the body's armpit. The blood is pumped out and another fluid is pumped in. This new chemical slows the decomposition process.

Embalmers use cotton balls to stuff the holes in the body. This stops fluids and gases from escaping. They use wax, clay, and stuffing to keep the body from deflating. Plastic disks are put under the eyelids. This hides the sinking eyeballs. Then the embalmer uses makeup to make the body look as lifelike as possible.

CHAPTER FOUR

PROCESSING MEAT

A meat processor is a worker who cuts up and kills livestock. The worker kills the animal with a stun gun and a slit is made in the animal's neck. This allows the blood to drain into a basin. The processor washes the animal. Then he or she cuts the belly open with a large electric saw.

The guts are removed, trimmed, and sorted. If the processor's cut is crooked, the guts could spill open. This could pour stomach juices everywhere.

The processor then cuts off the animal's head. He or she peels off its skin. Then the processor shaves or burns the hair off the skin. He or she splits the animal into smaller parts with a band saw. Finally, the processor wraps the smaller bits of meat in plastic and ships it all to the butcher.

Butchers work in shops or grocery stores. They use knives, grinders, and meat saws to cut up the meat. Then they cut away the parts that no one wants to eat. This includes the veins and bits of fat. A knife is used to remove the meat from the bone. The butcher cuts meat into portions. He or she wraps the trimmed meat in clear plastic. Then the butcher sets the meat out in chilled display cases for the shoppers to buy. If the fresh meat does not sell, the butcher must throw it out.

meat grinder

CHAPTER FIVE

HANDLING DEAD ANIMALS

When an animal is killed after being hit by a vehicle, a roadkill collector comes in. The worker will use a shovel to scrape the animal off the ground. He or she picks up bones and guts. The rest of the blood and bits of hair are washed away. Sometimes, the **remains** are given to a taxidermist.

Taxidermists turn animal remains into a display. They cut the dead animal open. Then they take out the guts and throw them away. Sometimes, if the animal died naturally, the remains fill up with gas like a balloon. The taxidermist must pop the carcass to let the gas escape.

The taxidermist carefully removes the skin. He or she boils the skinless body. This causes all the meat to fall off the bones.

remains — parts that are left when an animal dies

Then the skin is put back onto the bones. Cotton balls and wax are used to pad the bones until the body looks lifelike. Glass eyeballs are put in the place of the animal's real eyeballs. The stuffed animal can be collected, sold, or donated to a museum.

CONCLUSION

THE WORKERS OF TODAY

Disgusting jobs are done every day. Roadkill collectors and taxidermists recycle dead animals. Meat processors kill and cut up animals for meat to feed people. The sewer workers and wastewater treatment plant workers make sure germ-filled poop and urine are handled safely.

When people die, coroners and embalmers handle the bodies. The bodies are then prepared for burial. If the bodies are not collected and treated right away, they can leave a mess. If there is a chance that a person died because of a crime, CSIs search the scene for evidence.

Disgusting jobs are dirty and dangerous. The hardworking men and women who do these jobs every day make the United States a safer and cleaner place.

> People at wastewater treatment plants work hard to provide clean water.

GLOSSARY

autopsy (AW-tahp-see) — when a body is cut open and studied to find out what caused the person's death

evidence (EV-i-duhns) — anything that can give a clue as to how an event happened

investigator (in-VES-ti-gate-or) — person who looks for clues to solve a mystery

leptospirosis (lep-toh-spahy-ROH-sis) — bacterial disease that humans can get from animals

morgue (MORG) — place where dead bodies are taken and stored; here they are either examined or sent to the embalmer to prepare for burial

remains (ri-MAYNS) — parts that are left when an animal dies

sewer (SOO-ur) — systems of underground pipes, tubes, and tunnels that connect together to move poop away from where people live

wastewater treatment plant (wayst-waw-tur TREET-ment plant) — facility where pollutants are taken out of dirty water

READ MORE

Bedell, J. M. *So, You Want to Work with Animals?* New York: Aladdin, 2017.

Flynn, Sarah Wassner. *This Book Stinks!* Washington, D.C.: National Geographic, 2017.

Mooney, Carla. *Forensics*. White River Junction, Vt.: Nomad Press, 2013.

INTERNET SITES

Use FactHound to find Internet sites related to this book.

Visit www.facthound.com

Type in this code: 9781543503661

CRITICAL THINKING QUESTIONS

1. Although some jobs in modern America involve disgusting tasks, how are they important to our society?
2. The jobs in this book are dangerous because they require exposure to deadly bacteria. Do you think a worker should be paid more for this increased risk of exposure? Why or why not?
3. Do you think technology will ever completely remove the need for people to do disgusting jobs? Why or why not?

INDEX

bacteria, 13
blood, 14, 17, 20, 21, 22, 26
bones, 25, 26, 28
bugs, 8, 11
butchers, 25

chemicals, 13, 21
coroners, 18, 19, 29
crime scene, 5, 14, 17, 29
CSIs, 4, 5, 14, 16, 29

diseases, 11

embalmers, 4, 21, 29
evidence, 14, 16, 20, 29

funeral homes, 5, 21

garbage, 8, 14

investigations, 5

meat processors, 22, 25, 29
medical examiner, 16, 20
morgue, 18

physicians, 4, 20
plumbing, 4
police, 18
poop, 4, 6, 8, 11, 12, 13, 29

rats, 11
roadkill collectors, 4, 26, 29

sewers, 4, 8, 11, 17

taxidermist, 26, 29
toilet, 6

urine, 4, 8, 11, 12, 29

wastewater treatment plant, 6, 13

ABOUT THE AUTHOR

After a unique childhood in the forests and islands of California, Jacque Summers earned a bachelor's degree in creative writing from Southern New Hampshire University. She teaches and writes about girls who made the past and will make the future. She is passionate about nature, evolution, and science.